Old IRVINE

by
David Pettigrew

Irvine centre, *c.*1900, dominated by the Town House. From here the town grew over the centuries and it was on the area of the High Street that the major redevelopments of the 1970s were centred. Some of the historic streets survived the bulldozers, notably Glasgow Vennel which has been preserved as it was when Robert Burns lived and worked there. This was the route taken by carts from the harbour to Glasgow. In 1781 Robert Burns set up a flax-dressing business at the street's Heckling Shop. Only 22 and yet to discover his poetic calling, his business there was a "soulless occupation", but after the shop was accidentally burned down he liked Irvine well enough to stay until March of 1782, while he sharpened his romantic talents and formed friendships with men such as the provost, Charles Hamilton, who later signed as guarantor for the Kilmarnock Edition.

The Old Tolbooth, Irvine.

Photo by T. Patterson, Irvine. J. R. R.—E.

© Stenlake Publishing 1997
First Published in the United Kingdom, 1997
By Stenlake Publishing, Ochiltree Sawmill,
The Lade, Ochiltree, Ayrshire KA18 2NX
Telephone/fax: 01290 423114

ISBN 1 872074 89 8

The first port at Irvine, at Townend near Seagate, attracted a population of fishermen, merchants and craftsmen and the community had developed enough by the end of the fourteenth century to require its own municipal centre. The Burgh Tolbooth was erected in the High Street beside the Merkat Cross in 1386 and housed the council chambers, the court house and the local prison (with walls four feet thick). Behind, stood the Tron, or municipal weighing machine. The Tolbooth pictured is the 1745 reconstruction of the original, demolished in 1860.

Introduction

In a 1308 charter from King Robert Bruce Irvine was already noted as a place of great antiquity, but the true age of the town is unknown.

Whatever settlement existed before records began, religion was a principal foundation for the community. Folklore says that babies came from under the 'Granny Stane' which lies in the River Irvine just beyond the bridge, but history suggests that this was once part of a circle of standing stones which stood in the approximate position of the weir and had a religious purpose. St Inan was probably preaching here in the ninth century and by the fourteenth Carmelite Friars were firmly established in the neighbouring parish of Fullarton.

The first record of the town's name is 1163 and even at this time Irvine's potential as a sea port was appreciated as the early Scottish kings extended their influence over the land. The sea washed right up to Seagate and the lands of Bogside (it did not recede until the fourteenth century) and a port, positioned at Townend near Seagate, was probably already in use at this time; a castle was erected nearby to protect it. By 1233 a church had been built on the site of the present parish kirk; church and castle assured Irvine's rapid development as a major town in medieval Ayrshire.

A royal burgh from the fourteenth century, Irvine was the main market town in the county of Ayr, enjoying superiority over both Ayr and Kilmarnock in matters of law and commerce. The county jail was in the Tolbooth and the local magistrates dispensed justice even on capital cases. The town also enjoyed the attention of various monarchs; James the IV passed through from time to time and Queen Mary allowed special jurisdiction to be given to the burgh council to help them contain the spread of the plague in the 1560s. Mary is strongly associated with the town and although the 3rd Earl of Eglinton was one of her advisers and she visited him at Eglinton, there is no evidence to suggest that she ever entered Irvine itself.

Until the eighteenth century, the town developed without hindrance. Industry and trade depended mainly on herring fishing, but it wasn't until the port was moved to the point of confluence between the rivers Irvine and Garnock in Fullarton that Irvine discovered a new prosperity.

By the early 1700s Irvine enjoyed status as Scotland's third largest seaport but this was in terms of ship tonnage and as the port of Irvine included all the small harbours from Largs to Troon including Arran, the claim cannot be taken too literally. Nevertheless, the harbour was used by Glasgow merchants for their flourishing tobacco trade with America and as coal was now being mined in outlying parts of the district, exports of this were being made to Ireland, France, Malta and Gibraltar. Imports included timber and grain from America, wine from France and butter from Ireland.

The opening of Port Glasgow dealt a heavy blow and a critical period followed. Irvine failed to establish its own industry and its status as the county's chief town fell away. Kilmarnock and Ayr quickly took the lead with textile manufacturing and Irvine's growth of population suddenly tailed off. The lean years continued until the mid-nineteenth century and weaving was the only significant industry. However, fortunes changed once more after 1850 when shipbuilding was begun at the docks and chemical manufactures were established at Fullarton by the river. Up the coast at Ardeer, Alfred Nobel opened his explosives factory and the harbour was given a boost as the shipping to and from here passed up the Garnock.

By 1921, when these industries had just passed their peak the town's population stood at 11,826. Housing was woefully inadequate and with the initiation of council housing schemes, Irvine began the long journey towards the New Town of today. It was calculated in 1948 that Irvine would need 1500 new houses but it was not until 1961 that the town finally had more rooms than people to fill them. Then in 1967, the Irvine Development Corporation was set up to oversee the development of Scotland's fifth New Town which would encompass Irvine, Kilwinning, Girdle Toll, Dreghorn and Drybridge and for better or worse, the old town of Irvine changed forever. The town centre was completely reconstructed; the bridge was demolished and rebuilt as a shopping centre which also devoured half of Bridgegate, while most of Fullarton was lost to shopping developments, high rise flats and council offices. However, 2,000 jobs were created as the new industrial estates attracted firms such as Hyster, Beechams and Volvo.

Twenty years later the New Town has fallen short of the high hopes of its conception. On the face of it the town appears to have remained a close-knit community but some say that the remodelled town centre lacks the atmosphere it once had. Industry, too, has had difficulties and many of the new jobs of the 1970s have since been lost. The 1976 Magnum Centre, once hailed as "the biggest leisure centre in Europe", faces competition from more recently built facilities in neighbouring towns and it seems that it was never immune to grumbles from some Irvinites that it was built too far from the town centre in the first place. Despite this, the recently preserved sites at Seagate and Glasgow Vennel, along with the new Scottish Maritime Museum complex, may yet prove to be valuable assets in facing the challenges of the next millenium.

The present parish church, built at Kirkgatehead in 1773, replaced an earlier chapel known as St Mary's. With a seating capacity of 1770, the building was nicknamed the 'Big Kirk'. At the end of the row on the right hand side of the picture is the burgh's first school, built in the 1570s but now demolished. Many of Irvine's historic figures received their education here, including author John Galt, lawyer David Boyle and for one year only (that's how long he was in town) Edgar Allan Poe, aged six. The progressive schoolmaster of the late eighteenth century provided an excellent literary curriculum and pupils could expect to study Milton, Bunyan, Pope and even Defoe and Swift.

Kirkgate, despite having been one of the town's most ancient streets was discarded in the overhaul of the 1960s and '70s. Originally, the street was known as Friarsgate until around 1540 when friars were becoming increasingly unfashionable. The Tolbooth dominated the street at that time.

Much of the row on the left has been demolished but one survivor is Scotland's first Orange Lodge, put up in 1872. In the middle and late nineteenth century religion in the town was in a state of flux; congregations at the Free Church splintered, the Roman Catholics were establishing themselves, and even the old Kirk saw a remarkable event - its first wedding - in 1881.

During the early centuries of the town's history, High Street ran only the length between Townhead and Bridgegate but was dominated by the Tolbooth around which the local markets were held. The street's central position continued with the building of the Town House in 1861 although long before this the street had grown far beyond Bridgegate. The statue commemorates David Boyle, the local man who became Lord Justice General of Scotland and sentenced Burke (of Burke and Hare) to death. The imposing structure often struck terror into the hearts of youngsters whose parents had told them that if they didn't behave the 'Black Man' would get them, although the urchins in the picture seem happy enough. The statue was moved out of sight to the foot of Seagate in 1929 and seems to have had its sooty exterior cleaned - the 'Black Man' is now green.

Boyle's statue was shifted because it was a hindrance to traffic, but the war memorial remained in its central position on High Street until 1952. In the years that it stood here it was the traditional site for the crowning of the Marymass Queen. This ceremony and indeed the 'queen' herself are actually recent additions to the Marymass fair, only introduced in 1928 in a successful attempt to revive a flagging festival. It was felt that the town's children were not being involved enough in the ceremonies and it was only at this time that the fair was consciously associated with Mary, Queen of Scots. The Marymass Queen was attended by other girls playing the 'four Marys', maids who were supposed to have accompanied Queen Mary on her (unlikely) visit to Seagate Castle.

THE CROSS, IRVINE.

A.4602

The approach to the Cross from High Street. Roughly located within this area was the original Merkat Cross, put up in the 1260s and which looked very like the war memorial. In early times all the town's business, proclamations and punishments took place here. Executions were held elsewhere but for crimes such as "horrid cursing", one could expect to be imprisoned in the Tolbooth and then be taken here to be pelted with rotten eggs. In 1694 the cross was taken down as it was considered as being "of an old fashion (and) doth mar the decorum of the street", an opinion not unlike the one held in the 1970s when half the town was ripped down and rebuilt in trendy concrete and glass.

The Cross viewed from the other end of High Street. The gable-ended building on High Street on the left of the picture was the Wheat Sheaf Inn, put up in the 1700s, and where the local freemasons of the time, including Robert Burns, met. Meetings now take place in the Masonic Lodge beside the cinema on Bank Street.

The view of the Cross from Bank Street, *c*.1900. The turreted building on the corner at the left was the Caledonian Arms, and later the Caledonian Halls used for meetings and dances. On page 8 it is shown housing the Coop drapery (their operation also included the drysaltery and butchers on Fullarton Place). At centre right is Saddler's Corner which was built in the 1830s and lasted until the great redevelopment. When it closed it was owned by Bob Couslar, president of the Carters Society, and many visitors to the shop will remember struggling to find him in the darkened premises, lost in the corner in a clutter of saddles and bridles.

HIGH STREET, IRVINE

Beyond the Cross lies the more recent half of High Street, which nevertheless contains two of Irvine's oldest pubs, the Eglinton Arms and the King's Arms Hotel. It was in the King's Arms that Prince Napoleon (later Napoleon III) of France stayed in 1839 while attending the Eglinton Tournament; in the same period it was also the meeting place for the fledgling Burns Club.

HIGH STREET, IRVINE.

A.527

A view of the same area from the 1950s. The tall building, by which the bus is parked, was built to replace an earlier tenement that was the birthplace of John Galt. The pictured building was itself knocked down to make way for the Bank of Scotland building and a plaque there commemorates the writer. Although the street is not particularly busy here, traffic congestion at the Cross and on the streets leading off it was intolerable and was eventually relieved by the opening of the Irvine by-pass and the Marress bridge over the river in 1973. Cars had always caused complaint however; in 1907 the council failed in a surprisingly far-sighted application to have 'dangerous and excessive speeds' limited to 10mph.

Although Marymass has been celebrated in one form or another since before recorded times, the pageantry of today's festival was only begun in the mid-17th century after the Town Council took responsibilty for its organisation. From that time on the fair always began with an opening ceremony performed by the local magistrates followed by a parade through the town by the town's officials and the carters.

The Carters Society have been involved in the celebrations from possibly as early as 1670 and since the 1750s the procession was always led by them to Irvine Moor where the carters horse race was run. From the 1850s the parade passed by the throng of sideshows and stalls which were ranged right along High Street. Fortune tellers and merry-go-rounds were the forerunners of the modern 'shows' and were immensely popular; they became so busy with revellers that they were eventually moved to the Moor in 1919 and then to the Golffields.

Back at the south end of town is Townhead, which looks, cobbles excepted, much the same today as it does here, although the YMCA building on the extreme right has gone. Until the late 17th century the town began on this end at High Street, flanked only by Kirk Vennel and Glasgow Vennel on the left and right. However, by 1700 Townhead had grown to almost three quarters the length of High Street itself as space was greedily consumed by the population of 1,500. Before this development the site had been sufficiently clear of inhabitants to allow the execution of local witches, twenty of whom were strangled and burned at the stake throughout the 1600s - even though a local scribe of the time described Irvinites as "very civill and weill cultured".

Seagate Castle, Irvine.

The castle on Seagate is Irvine's most ancient remaining structure. As late as the sixteenth century the sea came right up to the foot of Seagate and the castle stood sentinel over the main route from the harbour into town. The building that stands today was designed as a mansion house and built in the mid-1500s by the Eglintons to replace a castle that stood there from possibly as early as 1200. The tower of this original castle was incorporated into the new house which became known as the 'Palace' as a result. It is probably untrue that Mary, Queen of Scots, visited the house in 1563 but like the supposed existence of a tunnel linking the castle with those of Stane and Dundonald and haunted by a ghostly piper, it is a myth that still persists in local folklore. In the eighteenth century the house fell into ruin and became the haunt of smugglers who were exploiting, amongst other things, a roaring trade in illegal whisky from Arran.

Eglinton Street, Irvine

At the head of Seagate begins Eglinton Street which started life as an extension of High Street towards Kilwinning in the early 1500s and was built up by 1700. For 200 years until it was demolished in the 1930s, the street's most famous landmark was the Elephant Arms Inn which served the 'middle class' professional workers who had started to live in the street by the late nineteenth century. This inn occupied a former barn which had been taken over by students of Glasgow University between 1645 and '47 who were escaping the plague that was then sweeping their city. The street also houses the present premises of the world's first Burns Club which was formed in 1826 by Burns' friends David Sillar and John MacKenzie. The wholesaler's on the right was later Lamont's the Grocers in the 1950s.

KILWINNING ROAD AND ROYAL ACADEMY ANNEX, IRVINE   A 4604

The now demolished Irvine Academy Annexe on Kilwinning Road, erected in 1932 in an attempt to relieve the pressure on the academy's roll of 500. The building blended well with the grand houses around it which had been appearing since the 1820s, built by the town's upper class of rich merchants in an attempt to get away from the bustling centre. No such luck for the inhabitants of the 1930s however, as the road was often the scene of pitched battles between the annexe pupils and those of the catholic school nearby. Years later the solution to the overcrowded classrooms arrived in the shape of the new million pound Royal Academy (initially called Ravenspark Academy) which opened further along this road in 1969.

Bank Street was not laid out until 1828 when it was decided that better access to the harbour was needed from the east. At first it was named Bank Street after a branch of the Ayr Bank situated there. It attracted the town's rich and a series of large houses were built. Despite this, Bank Street was never as exclusive as Kilwinning Road, due to its proximity to the town centre and the unpleasnt premises of the Irvine Gas Light Company whose works began 136 years of production in nearby Ballot Road in 1829.

Bank Street and Bridgegate, Irvine

Bank Street was designed as a long thoroughfare and, nearer the town centre, businesses and shops were opened as well as places of entertainment. George Green's cinema opened in 1912, satisfying an appetite for films already whetted by the travelling filmshow that had camped on Low Green the year before. His cinema could seat 920 but later had to compete with the Picture Palace on Bridgegate which opened in 1920. The George burned down in 1969 and was rebuilt as the WMR Film Centre in 1976 - the opening show was *The Towering Inferno*. Pietro Pieroni's Cafe served fish and chips and ice cream to the picture goers and during the depression this particular cafe provided cheap fish suppers three times a week to the town's unemployed workforce. This service was briefly forgotten in 1940 when Italy's entry into the war caused riots in which local Italian shops were vandalised and looted.

Bank Street, Irvine.

From 1890 Irvine enjoyed the luxury of two railway stations; the first at Montgomery Street belonging to G&SWR, followed by the opening of the Caledonian Line from Kilwinning which terminated in Bank Street. It was hoped that this would lead to industrial developments on the east side of town but the necessary investments were never made. As a result the line was never very profitable, and such was the popularity of Kilwinning that most services consisted of a single carriage. Educational developments, however, did take place on Bank Street with the opening of the school there in 1875. The academy had been hard-pressed to meet the requirements of the town's children and until this school opened it had been running classes of up to 80 pupils.

Muir Drive from Dorian's, Irvine

By 1914 industries such as shipbuilding and chemical manufacturing were attracting a new workforce to the town. The population had swelled to around 10,000 and housing was severly wanting. Older tenements were decaying and overcrowded and some families were even living in vans on the street. The council decided to build in areas such as Kirk Vennel and behind Bank Street and also decided to set up an electricity supply. But it would take time; the houses on Muir Drive for example were not completed until 1921 and it was only by the 1930s that most houses, old and new, had electricity.

PICTURE PALACE

ALL KINDS OF REPAIRS

BRIDGEGATE, IRVINE

Although the first bridge at Irvine was probably built in the 14th century, the first record of one is in the following century at which time Bridgegate appeared as the street connecting it with the Cross and the High Street. Initially, there were actually gates at the bridge which were closed at night and reopened at five in the morning. By 1819 it was one of the town's principal streets and fully built up.

BRIDGEGATE, IRVINE.

B.3217.

The picture on this and the previous page show the street ten or twenty years apart. In 1920 the principal attraction was the cheap Picture Palace, although by the '40s the population's growing affluence is apparent from the radio dealer and jeweller shop. The Palace closed in 1957 and by the 1960s the street was suffering from dilapidated buildings and a narrowness which was causing severe traffic congestion onto the bridge. In 1972 the clearing began and the most radical changes in the town centre took place here as the old buildings were almost entirely swept away to make way for Bridgegate House and the pedestrianised shopping square.

Fifty yards further down towards the bridge and the area taken up by the Rivergate Centre of the 1970s and then further built upon by the Forum Mall of 1984. The turning on the left led to Rottenrow which itself joined with Chapel Lane, otherwise known as the Grip. Until the turn of the eighteenth century a loch lay immediately to the east of the burgh and from this ran a stream to the river, passing through the town parallel to Bridgegate. This was built upon to become the Grip and subsequently the stream became an open sewer until the loch was drained. Rottenrow no doubt shared certain characteristics with its neighbouring lane.

The reconstruction of the 1970s was not the first for Bridgegate. In the 1880s most of the right hand side of the street was pulled down to make way for the buildings above. The one survivor was the Bridge Hotel which enjoyed a seventy year stay of execution until fire ended its days in the 1950s.

The cavernous premises of Colvin's general store, which took the place of the Post Office and shops pictured on the previous page. In the intervening period the building seems to have taken the name of 'The Polytechnic' although it never housed any of Irvine's schools. The monicker made Mr Colvin's premises seem that little bit more special than anywhere else, after all he had the Coop to contend with. A similar trick was used by the famous Glasgow department store, John Anderson's Royal Polytechnic.

Ross's garage and car showroom was positioned at the end of Bridgegate in the place of the cottage on the right of Page 25, and stood opposite the Bridge Hotel and Yule's undertakers. It was also known as Shaw's Garage at one time and later became first a furniture store then an electrical goods shop before closure in the 1970s. The premises may look quite compact but stretched back into another building positioned behind it on the river bank. Other businesses on Bridgegate included Short's Bakery, home of the famous pies.

Irvine, 1922. Six of the town's seven churches are on display here and of the most interest is the Relief Church of 1773, the roof of which can be seen to the left of the second church (the Mure Church) from the foreground. This church was built for a splinter-group of the parish congregation who 'walked out' in outrage after the Earl of Eglinton presented a new minister without first conferring on the choice with them; the new church 'relieved' them from the oppressive noble. It was from this church that the famous Buchanites emerged. Founded by Elizabeth Buchan, self-styled "wonder of heaven", this extremist group gathered as a sort of commune in a house on Glasgow Vennel and practised a confused religion which effectively boiled down to 'free love' amongst its members. Burns wrote of their 'great farce of pretended devotion' and in 1784 they were driven from the town by outraged Irvinites. They left town proclaiming their journey to the new Jerusalem, which apparently lay in Kircudbrightshire, reached via Kilmarnock.

The bridge viewed from Waterside. This one was built in 1745, but previous to the first bridge of the fourteenth century was a river crossing between the burghs of Irvine and Fullarton at Puddleford, below the Parish Church on the other side of the bridge shown here. Here William Wallace (who has since been incorporated into the Marymass procession) is supposed to have enjoyed one of his many skirmishes with English soldiers. Puddleford is also possibly the site of the local ducking stool, used to try witches. More recently, a Bailey bridge was strung across the water here as part of the military operations in the town during WWII.

On the right stands the Trinity Church, erected on Mizer Hill in 1863. Closed in 1966, the building is now a community centre but is one of only three remiaining examples of the gothic style of its architect F.T. Pilkington.

Montgomery Street, Irvine.

Montgomery Street used to reach as far as Fullarton Place (which begins at the tea shop on the right), almost as far as the bridge itself. Originally known as the Halfway, the street was renamed in 1882 after the 'christian poet' James Montgomery, born there a century earlier.

Montgomery Street, Irvine.

Industry proliferated at the harbour and the surrounding area in the late nineteenth century and Montgomery Street was amongst the liveliest in Irvine. Most of the workers from the new shipyards and chemical works lived here in 1900 and the tightly-packed streets of Fullarton contained half of the town's population of nearly 10,000.

MONTGOMERY STREET, IRVINE

Montgomery Street, looking up from the approximate position of the railway station. To the right, past the Gushet House is Loudon Street since demolished for the development of the Riverway Retail Park. At the time of these pictures (c1900) the town was taking on a certain roughness, with working men drinking at the weekends and crime on the increase. The Argyle Inn was just one of the 65 pubs in town. In Ayrshire, only Kilwinning had more.

Fullarton Street, Irvine.

Fullarton Street was nicknamed 'Soor Milk Row' as some residents had painted their houses with whitewash mixed with sour milk for added adhesion. The burgh of Fullarton was established in 1707 and the street was laid in 1776. The area was a community in itself and by 1820 its population was over 1,900. By the early years of the twentieth century the street housed workers of the nearby naptha and Watt's ropeworks and had degenerated into a slum. Poor housing and overcrowding were for most of the pre- and post-Second World War period a serious problem for the town council and combated with a council housing programme. In 1968 much of this street was cleared for the building of the five tower blocks which now dominate the Irvine skyline.

Fullarton was one of the religious centres of early Irvine. From the fourteenth century until the 1560s there was a Carmelite Friary known as Friar's Croft (later a streetname in the immediate vicinity), roughly on the site of today's Cunninghame House. Set up by the Fullarton family, its comforts were such that King James IV occasionally came to stay.

On the left is Fullarton Free Church, built on Church Street in 1836. Not long after the congregation was established it splintered and a separate church was formed and housed in a specially built hall on the riverside nearby. Known as the Wilson Fullarton Church, it was a much grander building than the one above. Today it has lost half its steeple and, dwarfed by the Rivergate centre, is merely the recreational hall for the original church.

LOW GREEN AND WATERSIDE, IRVINE.   98624.

Waterside was another select street for the town's merchants but in winter the river was prone to flooding and the residents were issued with sand bags to protect their properties from the rising torrent. In 1897 the weir was built further downstream and this part of the river then became popular with bathers and boaters. Building of the weir provoked some controversy due to the removal of ancient boulders said to be the remains of the standing stones around which Irvine originated. Despite public disapproval they were removed anyway as the weir had been one of the council's long-cherished plans.

The Academy seen here under construction in 1900, was built on the site of the first academy of 1816, which had opened after the Kirkgate school had become too small. This itself became too small and even the new academy failed to solve the problem of overstuffed classrooms. In 1913 Bank Street school still had over 600 pupils and eventually the annexe on Kilwinning Road had to be built. The Academy had three entrances; there were two at either side for pupils and staff while the one at the front was reserved solely for the rector.

The Race Course. Bogside. Irvine.

M. 147.

The racecourse at Bogside was opened by the 12th Earl of Eglinton in 1807 and the principal annual meet was during the last three days of June when all the nobles and gentry of Ayrshire attended. In 1838, Scotland's first steeplechase was run here as was the Scottish Grand National from 1947 to 1965 when the course closed. Irvine is one of the homes of horse racing; an event has been held at the time of Marymass for possibly the last 1000 years and the carters established their own 'Cadger's course' on the Moor by the late eighteenth century.

The town from the south. The wood on the right formed part of the Golffields, which along with the Moor and Bogside were municipal lands used for events such as Marymass. Pronounced 'Go-fields', the area has been known in the past as Goatfields and Goalfields and seems never to have had a link with with golf. In the 1600s the farmland was rented out on short-term lets to locals wanting to grow their own produce. In the nineteenth century the town wash house was there and later a bleaching works. Cricket was also played there in a craze for the game which lasted until the 1920s. From around 1920 until 1973 the Marymass shows were staged here until they moved back to the Moor. Today the area is almost entirely built up but the name lives on with Golffields Road.

GLASGOW HIGHLANDERS GAILES 1909

A battalion of Glasgow Highlanders at Gailes Camp in 1909. During both world wars large numbers of troops were billeted here and at the Moor where in the second war Polish troops were stationed. They fraternised with the locals but were generally treated with suspicion due to specious rumours that their numbers included Germans posing as Poles, supposedly to avoid capture by the Allies back in Europe. Their unpopularity was confirmed after an incident one evening at the Tivoli Dance Hall (later the Ritz) when, in a fight over a girl, a Pole slashed a Scottish soldier. When word got round the locals were so incensed that they prepared to march on the Moor to teach the foreigners a lesson. They were thwarted by the police however, who had to barricade the High Street with buses to block their access to the Moor.

Camp Stores, Meadow Park.

CAMP - STORES

During the inter-war years this chalet camp was set up near Gailes and consisted of around 200 huts owned by Glaswegians who came down the coast for their holidays. Other amenities included a dance hall. The Caledonia Paper factory, which can be seen from the A78 to Troon, stands on its site today. Information about the place is sparse, suffice to say that this card was sent in 1936 by an employee of the camp called Dorothy who explained that life there was "very full and interesting", no doubt in anticipation of the nudist colony which would later appear in the vicinity.

THE SANDS, IRVINE.

A.7365.

Despite the example of Meadow Park, the town council repeatedly failed to realise the potential of Irvine beach as a holiday resort in the 1930s. At that time the area was still taken up by factories such as ICI, opened on Gailes (now Portland) Road in 1935 (the chimneys overshadowing the beach probably belonged to these works) and the Portland Glass Company (now Rockware) which opened in 1920. In those years Irvine may have been enjoying a short-term boom as one of Ayrshire's major industrial centres but competing towns such as Saltcoats and Ayr were busy exploiting their coastal positions as holiday resorts, an area of revenue not fully understood by the town's administrators until the 1960s, by which time the Spanish holiday boom had started.

THE SANDS, IRVINE.

The mixture of leisure and work activity going on in this beach scene illustrates the council's failure to understand the value of the beach in an age of cheap bus and train travel. Working men and families alike are enjoying the good weather, but these are all undoubtedly local people. Campers were not welcome here; indeed as late as the 1950s tourists were being evicted from their campsites on the beach. On the other hand the pollution into the sea from shipping and chemical works, not to mention the waste washing its way down the Garnock from Ardeer, was probably appalling and not likely to entice crowds of swimmers to frolick in the effluent.

SIGNAL TOWER AND BATHING STATION, IRVINE

In 1927 the council did make one concession to beach recreation when they approved the opening of the bathing hut, pictured on the right. This was actually the tatty old lifeboat shed - hardly the Magnum by any stretch of the imagination. On the left is the Signalling Tower, invented by harbour master Martin Boyd in 1911, and unique to Irvine. It was designed to automatically signal the depth of the sea at the bar by a cock and ball system connected to the signalling balls on the mast.

Irvine Lifeboat crossing the Bar.

By the 1860s, exports from the harbour were only of coal and Irvine lost to Troon its place as the county's main port. Nevertheless, it retained its lifeboat station which had been set up in 1835. As the years went on the fishing fleet disappeared and by 1914 there were practically no local fishermen and no experienced sailors to man the lifeboat.

Seventeenth century Irvine enjoyed a healthy trade with Ireland and Europe. French wines, salt from Spain, cloth from Holland, and Scandinavian timber and iron were all imported. In return Irvine exported hides, wool, coal and principally herring and salmon. Success was such that a new port was built beyond Halfway on the mouth of the Garnock in 1677 (access to the old port had often been blocked by sand). By 1760 Irvine could boast of being Scotland's third port in terms of tonnage of ships, behind only Port Glasgow and Leith; indeed even after Port Glasgow was built, but before Glasgow itself became a seaport, the harbour was used by the tobacco barons to receive small American shipments.

THE HARBOUR, IRVINE.   98626.

Trade inevitably took a downward turn after Port Glasgow was opened and Irvine faced stiff local competition from the ports at Ayr, Ardrossan and Troon. By the late 1700s the town had failed to develop a significant industry of its own to replace the lost Glasgow business and the port had to rely on fishing and exports of coal to Ireland. This was mined at pits throughout the surrounding area from Kilwinning to Dundonald, although not in the town itself (a mine sunk on Low Green in 1762 was short-lived). The carters were responsible for the transport of coal from the pits to the harbour and their society organized a system of tariffs for cart rental. Their contribution is commemorated by a superb bronze sculpture on Harbour Street. The 'mountain' in the background here is actually a slag tip of waste accumulated from the various factories known as the Blue Billy Bing.

Irvine Harbour.

In 1750 Irvine had been the leading town in the county, but the census of 1850 shows just how far the town had fallen behind Kilmarnock and Ayr. A population of 7,500 could hardly compete with Kilmarnock's 21,400 or Ayr's 17,600 and this number would drop even further as the brief cotton industry died away, reducing the town to weaving and ropemaking. However, the situation improved again in 1871 with the opening of Henderson's chemical works and from 1886 shipbuilding became a major concern, although it was a slow starter as the first yard had opened in 1759. It reached its peak around 1912 when 1000 men, mostly from the Fullarton side of the river, were employed there building ships of up to 10,000 tons.

It was a short-lived boom and most of the heavy industries went into decline in the 1920s. In 1937 the shipyards lauched their last ship. However refitting and repairs continued after they were bought by National Shipbuilding Securities Ltd. In the '50s the yards again changed management, this time to the Ayrshire Dockyard Company, and produced prefabricated sections for ships until Ayrshire Metals Ltd bought the site in 1961. They are still in business today.

Shipbuilding demanded the manufacture of metal parts and this motley crew are likely to be at Laird's Forge on Guthries (now Gottries) Road. They were known simply as the Blockworks as they made block and tackle for ships and the iron hooks to go with them. They also made ship's wheels and apparatus for boats such as the QEII and branched out into the manufacture of coal cutting equipment. This business later became Bonnyforge International and only closed as recently as 1982. Other Irvine metalworks included Flanagan's Brassworks on Cochrane Street and Kerr's Forge next to the playing fields behind Bank Street.

THE HARBOUR, IRVINE.

A.524

Responsible for the controversial redevelopments of the 1970s, the Irvine Development Corporation trod a safer path in their work on the harbour area which was one of their last projects before their dissolution at the end of 1996. Much of the harbour and Harbour Street has been preserved and a large part of the site makes up the Scottish Maritime Museum which was also involved in the regeneration. New buildings have been sensitively designed to provide a gentle contrast with the existing architecture and with this complex, Irvine has finally realised its potential as a resort.

Bensley

The old town of Irvine is not the only place to have seen changes in the last few decades. The boundary of the New Town encompasses the sites of a number of old villages which have mostly disappeared under more recent housing schemes. Bensley is one such place and lay in the Girdle Toll area. All that is left is a cottgae and small church but the hamlet is remembered by Bensley Rise and Bensley Avenue. It was a collection of miners rows, established in 1846 and owned by the coalmaster A. Finnie who probably gave the men work at Fergushill Coliery near Kilwinning. This view may look idyllic but conditions were basic; there was only one spring water pump and the 57 stone houses were provided only with earth closets which were shared between four households.

The Eglinton family were associated with Irvine almost from its beginnings and they occupied the Eglinton Estate for over 700 years. The house above was built between 1796 and 1802 by Hugh, the 12th Earl (creator of Bogside race course) on the site of the thirteenth century Montgomerie Castle which had been sacked in 1527 by the Cunninghames of Kilmaurs druing a feud which lasted 100 years. The high point in the estate's history was the Tournament of 1839. Disappointed by the lack of pomp and pageantry at Queen Victoria's coronation two years earlier, the 13th Earl decided to hold an event which would recall the sights and sounds of medieval chivalry and so over two days, events such as jousts with knights in authentic costumes entertained up to 100,000 spectators. Within a century however, this grand estate was wracked by debt and the family abandoned the castle, which then quickly fell into ruin. Its destruction was assured by the Royal Enginners who, during the war, practised demolition tactics on it. Nevertheless, the IDC initiated work on the estate which will eventually restore the lands to the way they were according to the 1750 plan book.

Celebrating

Chinese New Year:

A Rich Tradition

Blooming Tree Culture Publishing Group

Author: Rachel Zhang

Chief Illustrators: Emily Song, Rachel Zhang

Assitant Illustrators: Pearl Wang, Greta Chang, Maximo Zhang

Cover Design: Michael Wu

Craft Photographer: Emily Song

Editor: Greta Chang

Assistant Editor: Isaac Zhang

Editor-in-Chief: Yufeng Tu

Library of Congress Cataloging-in-Publication Data
Control Number: 2018931246

ISBN   978-1-5136-3161-5 (Paperback)

Chinese New Year, also known as "Spring Festival", is celebrated every year by nearly a quarter of the world's population. There are over 1.3 billion people in China who celebrate Chinese New Year. Several other counties celebrate Chinese New Year too.

Other Countries That Celebrate Chinese New Year

 Indonesia

 Malaysia

 North Korea

 Philippines

 Singapore

 Brunei

 South Korea

 Vietnam

Chinese New Year falls on the first day of the lunar calendar, which is based on the phases of the moon.

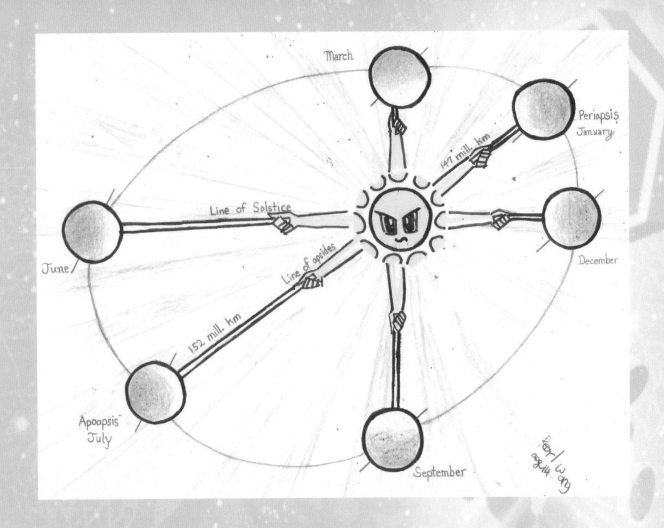

The solar calendar measures the Earth's rotation around the Sun. A year on the solar calendar has an average of 365.24 days while a year on the lunar calendar has only 354 days. To prevent the lunar calendar from deviating much from the solar calendar, a leap month is added to the lunar calendar every 32 or 33 months.

Each year on the lunar calendar has its own Zodiac sign. There are twelve animals in the Zodiac cycle. For example, the Zodiac sign for the year 2018 is Dog.

The exact date of Chinese New Year varies every year. However, it is always in January or February.

Before New Year starts, hundreds of millions of people travel to their hometown to reunite and gather with their family and friends. They usually go back home after the celebration. It is quite remarkable, for it is known as the largest human migration in the world*, also known as the Chinese Rush Period.

* John Kang and Yue Wang, World's largest human migration begins: Chinese New Year 2017, Forbes, 1/26/2017

A week before the new year begins, people start cleaning their houses, organizing their homes, donating and giving away items they no longer need, and settling debts as much as possible. A new year is a fresh start by turning over a new leaf.

Similar to the western tradition for Christmas, Chinese New Year celebrators also decorate their homes. They hang lanterns, stick window decorations, and put up calligraphy on red paper to bring prosperity.

An important dish to eat during New Year is dumplings. It is a must-have food on New Year's Eve. Similar to ravioli, the dumplings are made with wheat flour and stuffed with fillings. Popular fillings include chicken with mushrooms, carrots with lamb, and pork with cabbages. Dumplings are a symbol of wealth and good fortune because they are shaped like gold ingots, an ancient form of Chinese currency.

Families in southern China may take part in fancy feasts. It usually consists of multiple courses, with dishes including spring rolls, a large fish, and rice cakes. The food served may not be what you expect from your local Chinese fast food restaurant.

During Chinese New Year, it is very important for people to pay respects to their kin, especially their elders. It is a great bonding experience for the entire family. Children would usually wear a new outfit for the New Year's celebration.

Like Christmas, families and friends exchange gifts during Chinese New Year. The most iconic gift is the red envelope. Inside the envelope is money. Usually it is given to children by elders, in hopes that children will be wealthy and successful in the future.

Nowadays, people exchange digital red envelopes via online messaging systems such as WeChat. According to Reuters, an international news agency, WeChat users send around 46 billion e-envelopes during the period of Chinese New Year annually.

Setting off firecrackers is one of the most exciting activities for children to take part in. They are usually lit in front of store fronts or homes. People believe that it will scare away evil spirits and bring blessings to everyone in the New Year.

Over the years, it has become a Chinese custom to watch the Spring Festival TV Gala, or the CCTV New Year's Gala. It is considered to be the most watched television program, with an estimated over 800 million viewers! It features musicals, comedic skits, drama, magic performances, and acrobatic stunts. It is spectacular!

In addition to watching fireworks and firecrackers, people also enjoy watching other traditional customs. This includes colorful lion dances, drumming, and other vivid local performances. It is quite a beautiful sight to behold.

On the fifteenth and last day of the New Year's celebration, people celebrate by indulging on a pleasantly sweet dessert: glutinous rice balls. It is usually filled with sugary black sesame. Chewy in texture, it is a delightful treat and a true example of comfort and warmth on a cold winter day.

Emily Song, age 9; Rachel Zhang, age 9

A famous folktale the Chinese are fond of telling their children during Chinese New Year is the story of *nian*. In ancient times, there was a terrible monster with a large head and long horns by the name of *nian*. It only showed up on New Year's Eve to terrorize people and eat their livestock. To stop the treacherous monster, people put up red paper on their walls and doors, wore red, lit candles and set off firecrackers to scare the monster away. These traditions endure to this day to ward off evil spirits.

The Plagues and the
PASSOVER

Blood of
Lamb

Chinese
Decoration

Chinese New Year tradition is similar to the Jewish Passover Celebration. In the Bible, to avoid the tenth plague, God told the Jews to smear blood on their doorposts so the angel of death would not harm them. To Jews, red symbolizes blood, and similar to Chinese culture, also represents blessing.

Angel of Death

Monster of *Nian*

Shabbat
Candles

Chinese
Lantern

Just like how the Shabbat candles bring
sanctity to the Jewish holidays, the Chinese
people believe that lanterns bring peace, light,
and warmth to the New Year celebration.

To wrap it all up, New Year's tradition is just a celebration to welcome the new year. Celebrate this beautiful time of year with a big smile! We wish you a happy and blessed and very auspicious New Year!

How to Make a Simple Lantern

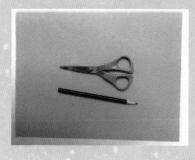

1) Use a letter-size paper and get your pencil and scissors ready.

2) Cut one inch of the paper and put it aside.

3) Fold the paper in half. Use a pencil to mark the folded part of the paper, inch by inch.

4) Cut the paper. Unfold and roll gently.

5) Put the two ends of the paper together and glue the paper along the edge.

6) Now you have your Chinese Lantern ready for the New Year!

Printed in Great Britain
by Amazon

36922702R00016